Magical Endings

from

Cool Whip ® Whipped Topping & **JELL-O** ® BRAND

Publications International, Ltd.

Favorite Brand Name Recipes at www.fbnr.com

ANGEL FLAKE, BAKER'S, CHIPS AHOY!, COOL WHIP, COUNTRY TIME, GERMAN'S, HONEY MAID, JELL-O, JET-PUFFED, LORNA DOONE, MAXWELL HOUSE, MYSTIC, NABISCO, NILLA, NUTTER BUTTER, OREO, PHILADELPHIA, PLANTERS, PLANTERS COCKTAIL and RITZ are registered trademarks of Kraft Foods Holdings.

BISQUICK is a registered trademark of General Mills, Inc.
BREYERS® is a registered trademark owned and licensed by Unilever, N.V.
DOLE is a registered trademark of Dole Food Company, Inc.

Kraft Kitchens Consumer Food Manager: Normajean Longfield

Photography: Stephen Hamilton Photographics, Inc.
Photographers: Stephen Hamilton, Tate Hunt
Photographers' Assistant: Tom Guida
Prop Stylist: Paula Walters
Food Stylists: Walter Moeller, Carol Smoler
Assistant Food Stylist: Susie Skoog

Pictured on the front cover *(clockwise from top left):* Christmas Rainbow Cake *(page 20),* JELL-O Yogurt Parfaits *(page 86),* Layered Mint-Chocolate Loaf *(page 56)* and Black & White Banana Pudding *(page 44).*

Pictured on the back cover: Cranberry-Orange Dream *(page 12).*

ISBN: 0-7853-7085-4

Manufactured in China.

8 7 6 5 4 3 2 1

Microwave Cooking: Microwave ovens vary in wattage. Use the cooking times as guidelines and check for doneness before adding more time.

Preparation/Cooking Times: Preparation times are based on the approximate amount of time required to assemble the recipe before cooking, baking, chilling or serving. These times include preparation steps such as measuring, chopping and mixing. The fact that some preparations and cooking can be done simultaneously is taken into account. Preparation of optional ingredients and serving suggestions is not included.

Magical Endings

from **Cool Whip** Whipped Topping & **JELL-O** BRAND

Holidays are a Special Time of the Year

The holidays are fast approaching, and I always look forward to getting together with family and friends. As busy as the holidays get, there's nothing more special than making all kinds of goodies. Whether it's that traditional family dessert or irresistible treats for friends, I know that I'll be in the kitchen whipping up one of these delightful recipes.

I know how hectic this time of the year is, so here in the Kraft Kitchens we've put together a fabulous collection of recipes that will delight your senses and make every day just a little bit sweeter for you and your loved ones.

Looking for that perfect dessert that is sure to wow everyone? The possibilities are endless. Choose from our decadent Frozen Black-Bottom-Peanut Butter Pie, festive Holiday Poke Cake, impressive Christmas Rainbow Cake and many more. By the time you have sampled every page, you will be well into the New Year.

So whether you're in the mood to please your family, impress friends or just satisfy your sweet tooth, you'll be sure to find it here. This cookbook brings you some of our best recipes and tips, but if you want more ideas, visit our web sites, *www.jell-o.com, www.coolwhip.com* or *www.kraftfoods.com,* where more creative ideas and recipes await you.

Each year people here in the Kraft Kitchens create new recipes that are perfect for every occasion. We are here to help make the holidays easier. So, gather your friends and family for some good times and good food.

I always welcome your comments; please write to me at *Stephanie@Kraftfoods.com.*

Stephanie

Stephanie Williams
Director Kraft Kitchens

6

Tips for Success with Cool Whip & Jell-O

Gelatin

• To make a mixture that is clear and uniformly set, be sure the gelatin is completely dissolved in boiling water or other boiling liquid before adding the cold water.

• To double the recipe, just double the amounts of gelatin, liquid and other ingredients used, except salt, vinegar and lemon juice. For these, use 1½ times the amount given in the recipe.

• To store prepared gelatin overnight or longer, cover it before refrigerating to prevent drying. Always store gelatin desserts and molds in the refrigerator.

• Generally, gelatin molds are best served right from the refrigerator. A gelatin mold containing fruit or vegetables can remain at room temperature up to 2 hours. Always keep a gelatin mold containing meat, mayonnaise, ice cream or other diary products refrigerated until ready to serve.

Pudding

• Stir mix-ins such as chopped candy bars, cookies, BAKER'S Semi-Sweet Chocolate Chunks, JET-PUFFED Miniature Marshmallows, chopped banana, chopped strawberries, raspberries, blueberries, chopped or drained canned fruit cocktail into prepared pudding just before serving.

Cool Whip

• Thaw COOL WHIP Whipped Topping completely before measuring or stirring into ingredients (see tub for how to thaw).

• COOL WHIP Whipped Topping can be scooped like ice cream directly from the tub while still frozen.

• Completely thawed COOL WHIP Whipped Topping can be spooned into a pastry bag or decorating tube and piped decoratively like whipped cream or frosting.

• Drain thawed frozen fruit before serving with COOL WHIP Whipped Topping. The juice may make the topping appear curdled.

• COOL WHIP Regular, Extra Creamy and COOL WHIP Lite Whipped Toppings can usually be interchangeable in recipes. When used with gelatin or high-acid fruits, COOL WHIP Lite may produce a softer set.

• COOL WHIP Free is not interchangeable with all the recipes in this magazine. When substituting COOL WHIP Free, the end result will be very soft set and slightly lower volume.

Cool Whip Whipped Topping & JELL-O® BRAND

Holiday Delights

JELL-O *Easy Relish*

2¼ cups orange juice
 ½ teaspoon ground cinnamon
 ⅛ teaspoon ground cloves
 1 package (4-serving size) JELL-O Brand Cranberry Flavor Gelatin
1½ cups finely chopped dried fruit and nuts (such as apricots, raisins, dates and PLANTERS Walnuts)

STIR juice, cinnamon and cloves in saucepan. Bring to boil; boil 3 minutes. Stir hot liquid into gelatin in large bowl at least 2 minutes until completely dissolved. Refrigerate about 1½ hours or until thickened (spoon drawn through leaves a definite impression). Stir in fruit and nut mixture.

REFRIGERATE about 1 hour or until cold. Spoon relish into serving bowl. Serve over ice cream, pound cake or with your holiday meal.

Variation: *Prepare as directed substituting JELL-O Brand Lemon or Orange Flavor Gelatin for the Cranberry Flavor.*

Prep Time: 15 minutes plus refrigerating

JELL-O Easy Relish

Frozen Pudding Tortoni

1²/₃ **cups cold half-and-half**
¹/₂ **teaspoon almond extract**
1 **package (4-serving size) JELL-O Vanilla Flavor Instant Pudding & Pie Filling**
2 **cups thawed COOL WHIP Whipped Topping**
¹/₄ **cup drained chopped maraschino cherries (optional)**
¹/₂ **cup chopped amaretti cookies (Italian almond-flavored cookies) *or* chopped toasted PLANTERS Slivered Almonds**

POUR half-and-half and almond extract into large bowl. Add pudding mix. Beat with wire whisk 2 minutes or until well blended. Gently stir in whipped topping. Stir in cherries and chopped cookies. Spoon into individual dessert dishes or paper-lined muffin cups.

FREEZE 3 hours or until firm.   *Makes 8 servings*

Great Substitute: *Use JELL-O Pistachio Flavor Instant Pudding instead of Vanilla Flavor. Garnish each serving with a dollop of thawed COOL WHIP Whipped Topping and additional chopped amaretti cookies, if desired.*

Prep Time: 10 minutes plus freezing

Tip

For a really festive holiday look, place colorful doilies or paper napkins on the plate under the tortoni.

Cranberry-Orange Dream

1½ cups boiling water
1 package (8-serving size) *or* 2 packages (4-serving size each) JELL-O Brand Cranberry Flavor Gelatin
1 can (16 ounces) whole berry cranberry sauce
1½ cups cold water
1 can (15.5 ounces) DOLE Mandarin Oranges, drained
1½ cups HONEY MAID Graham Cracker Crumbs
½ cup sugar, divided
½ cup (1 stick) butter *or* margarine, melted
1 package (8 ounces) PHILADELPHIA Cream Cheese, softened
2 tablespoons milk
2 tubs (8 ounces each) COOL WHIP Whipped Topping, thawed, divided

STIR boiling water into gelatin in large bowl at least 2 minutes until completely dissolved. Stir in cranberry sauce until melted. Stir in cold water. Refrigerate about 1¼ hours or until slightly thickened (consistency of unbeaten egg whites). Gently stir in mandarin oranges.

MEANWHILE, stir crumbs, ¼ cup of the sugar and butter in 13×9-inch baking dish. Firmly press onto bottom. Refrigerate until ready to fill.

BEAT cream cheese, remaining ¼ cup sugar and milk in large bowl with wire whisk until smooth. Gently stir in 1 tub of the whipped topping. Spread evenly over crust. Spoon gelatin mixture over cream cheese layer.

REFRIGERATE 3 hours or until firm. Just before serving, spread or dollop with remaining tub whipped topping.
Makes 16 servings

Helpful Hint: *Soften cream cheese in microwave on HIGH 15 to 20 seconds.*

Prep Time: 25 minutes plus refrigerating

Double Chocolate & Cinnamon Bread Pudding

2 packages (4-serving size each) JELL-O Chocolate Flavor Sugar Free Cook & Serve Pudding & Pie Filling (not Instant)
5 cups fat free milk
2 teaspoons ground cinnamon
5 cups French bread cubes
1 package (4 ounces) BAKER'S GERMAN'S Sweet Baking Chocolate, chopped

HEAT oven to 350°F.

STIR pudding mixes and milk in large bowl with wire whisk 1 minute or until well blended. Add cinnamon and whisk until thoroughly combined. Stir in bread. Pour pudding mixture into 13×9-inch baking dish. Sprinkle evenly with chopped chocolate.

BAKE 40 minutes or until pudding just comes to a boil in the center. Remove from oven. Let stand 10 minutes before serving. Serve warm.   *Makes 12 servings*

Special Extra: *Garnish pudding with COOL WHIP LITE or COOL WHIP FREE Whipped Topping.*

How to make individual servings: *Make individual servings of bread pudding by baking in custard cups or ramekins. Reduce baking time to 15 to 20 minutes.*

Dalmatian Bread Pudding: *Substitute JELL-O Vanilla Flavor Sugar Free Cook & Serve Pudding & Pie Filling for Chocolate Flavor Pudding & Pie filling to create a delicious black and white bread pudding.*

Prep Time: 15 minutes
Bake Time: 40 minutes

Easy Holiday Trifle

4 cups boiling water
1 package (8-serving size) *or* **2 packages (4-serving size each) JELL-O Brand Orange Flavor Gelatin**
1 package (8-serving size) *or* **2 packages (4-serving size each) JELL-O Brand Cranberry Flavor Gelatin**
2 cups cold water
1 package (10.75 ounces) frozen pound cake, thawed and cubed
1 tub (8 ounces) COOL WHIP Whipped Topping, thawed
2 cups sliced strawberries (optional)

STIR 2 cups boiling water into each flavor of gelatin in separate bowls at least 2 minutes until completely dissolved. Stir 1 cup cold water into each bowl. Pour into separate 13×9-inch baking pans. Refrigerate 3 hours or until firm. Cut each pan into ½-inch cubes.

PLACE cranberry gelatin cubes in 3½-quart serving bowl or trifle bowl. Layer with cake cubes, ½ of the whipped topping and strawberries. Cover with orange gelatin cubes. Garnish with remaining whipped topping.

REFRIGERATE at least 1 hour or until ready to serve.
Makes 12 to 15 servings

How To Serve: *This recipe can also be made in individual glasses as parfaits. Proceed as directed above, alternating gelatin cubes, cake cubes, strawberries and whipped topping.*

Prep Time: 20 minutes plus refrigerating

Tip

To make a lower calorie version, try substituting angel food cake for the pound cake, and use sugar free gelatin and COOL WHIP FREE.

JELL-O *& Juice Holiday Mold*

2½ cups boiling water
1 package (8-serving size) *or* **2 packages (4-serving size each) JELL-O Brand Strawberry Flavor Gelatin** *or* **any red flavor**
1 cup cold orange juice *or* **cranberry juice cocktail**
1 can (8 ounces) pineapple chunks, drained
1 can (11 ounces) mandarin orange segments, drained

STIR boiling water into gelatin in large bowl at least 2 minutes until completely dissolved. Stir in cold juice. Refrigerate about 1½ hours or until thickened (spoon drawn through leaves definite impression).

STIR in fruit. Spoon into 6-cup mold or bowl which has been sprayed with no stick cooking spray.

REFRIGERATE 4 hours or until firm. Unmold. Garnish as desired.   *Makes 10 servings*

Note: *Do not use fresh or frozen pineapple, kiwi, papaya or guava juice. Gelatin will not set.*

How To Unmold: *Dip mold in warm water for about 15 seconds. Gently pull gelatin from around edges with moist fingers. Place moistened serving plate on top of mold. Invert mold and plate; holding mold and plate together, shake slightly to loosen. Gently remove mold and center gelatin on plate.*

Prep Time: 10 minutes plus refrigerating

Spiced Cranberry Raisin Pie

2 cups fresh *or* frozen cranberries
½ cup cinnamon-flavored raisins
¾ cup sugar
1 cup apple juice *or* water
1 teaspoon grated orange peel
2 tablespoons cornstarch
¼ cup cold water
1 package (4-serving size) JELL-O Brand Gelatin, any red flavor
1 HONEY MAID Honey Graham Pie Crust (9 inch)
COOL WHIP Whipped Topping, thawed, for garnish

MIX cranberries, raisins, sugar, apple juice and orange peel in medium saucepan. Bring to boil over medium-high heat. Boil until cranberries start to pop. Mix cornstarch and water. Stir into cranberry mixture. Return to boil; boil 1 minute, stirring constantly. Remove from heat. Stir in gelatin until completely dissolved. Pour into crust.

REFRIGERATE 4 hours or until firm. Garnish with whipped topping. *Makes 8 servings*

Great Substitute: *Raisins and 1 teaspoon ground cinnamon can be substituted for the cinnamon-flavored raisins.*

Prep Time: 15 minutes plus refrigerating

Tip

This recipe is delicious with raspberry or strawberry flavor gelatin as well!

Frozen Pumpkin Squares

1 cup NABISCO Old Fashioned Ginger Snaps, finely crushed
¼ cup finely chopped PLANTERS Walnuts
¼ cup (½ stick) butter *or* margarine, melted
1¼ cups cold milk
2 packages (4-serving size each) JELL-O Vanilla Flavor Instant Pudding & Pie Filling
1 cup canned pumpkin
1 teaspoon pumpkin pie spice
1 tub (8 ounces) COOL WHIP Whipped Topping, thawed, divided

MIX crumbs, walnuts and butter in small bowl. Reserve 2 tablespoons for garnish. Press onto bottom of foil-lined 8-inch square pan. Refrigerate.

POUR milk into large bowl. Add pudding mixes, pumpkin and spice. Beat with wire whisk 2 minutes or until well blended. Gently stir in 2¼ cups of the whipped topping. Spread over crust.

FREEZE 4 hours or until firm. Let stand at room temperature 10 minutes or until dessert can be easily cut. Cut into squares. Garnish with remaining whipped topping and sprinkle with reserved crumbs.   *Makes 9 servings*

How To: *For easy snacking, wrap frozen squares individually and freeze. Take out as desired for quick snacks!*

Prep Time: 15 minutes
Freeze Time: 4 hours

Tip

For an extra special twist, stir ground cinnamon into COOL WHIP *before garnishing dessert.*

Frozen Pumpkin Square

Christmas Rainbow Cake

1 package (2-layer size) white cake mix
1 package (4-serving size) JELL-O Brand Lime Flavor
    Gelatin
1 package (4-serving size) JELL-O Brand Strawberry
    Flavor Gelatin
2 tubs (8 ounces each) COOL WHIP Whipped Topping,
    thawed

HEAT oven to 350°F.

PREPARE cake mix as directed on package. Divide batter equally between 2 bowls. Add lime gelatin to one bowl and strawberry gelatin to the other bowl. Stir until well blended. Pour each color batter into separate greased and floured 9-inch round cake pans.

BAKE 25 to 30 minutes or until toothpick inserted in center comes out clean. Cool 10 minutes; remove from pans. Cool to room temperature on wire racks.

SLICE each cooled cake layer in half horizontally. Place 1 lime-flavored cake layer on serving plate; frost with whipped topping. Top with 1 strawberry-flavored cake layer; frost with whipped topping. Repeat layers. Frost top and side of cake with remaining whipped topping.

Makes 10 to 12 servings

Storage Know-How: *Store cakes frosted with COOL WHIP Whipped Topping in the refrigerator.*

Great Substitute: *Use any two flavors of JELL-O Brand Gelatin to fit your favorite holiday.*

Prep Time: 30 minutes
Bake Time: 30 minutes

Christmas Rainbow Cake

No Bake Pumpkin Cheesecake Bars

1 package (11.1 ounces) JELL-O No Bake Real *or* Homestyle Cheesecake
¾ cup finely chopped PLANTERS Walnuts, divided (optional)
2 tablespoons sugar
6 tablespoons butter *or* margarine, melted
1 tablespoon water
1 cup cold milk
1 cup canned pumpkin
½ teaspoon pumpkin pie spice

STIR Crust Mix, ¼ cup walnuts, sugar, butter and water thoroughly in 8- or 9-inch square baking pan until crumbs are well moistened. Firmly press crumbs onto bottom of pan, using small measuring cup.

POUR milk into large bowl. Add pumpkin, Filling Mix and pumpkin pie spice. Beat with electric mixer on lowest speed until blended. Beat on medium speed 3 minutes. (Filling will be thick.) Spoon onto crust. Top with remaining walnuts.

REFRIGERATE at least 1 hour or until set. Cut cheesecake into squares.   *Makes 8 servings*

How To Serve: *To make cheesecake easier to serve, line 8- or 9-inch square pan with foil extending over edges to form handles. To serve, run knife around edges of pan to loosen cheesecake from sides. Lift cheesecake, using foil as handles, onto cutting board.*

Prep Time: 15 minutes plus refrigerating

Cranberry Pineapple Dessert

1½ cups boiling water
½ teaspoon ground cinnamon
1 package (8-serving size) *or* 2 packages (4-serving size) JELL-O Brand Cranberry Flavor Gelatin
2 cups cold water
1 can (20 ounces) DOLE Pineapple Chunks in Juice, drained

STIR boiling water and cinnamon into gelatin in large bowl at least 2 minutes until completely dissolved. Refrigerate 15 minutes. Stir in cold water. Refrigerate about 30 minutes or until slightly thickened (consistency of unbeaten egg whites). Gently stir 15 seconds. Reserve ¼ cup pineapple. Stir in remaining pineapple. Pour into 6-cup bowl.

REFRIGERATE 4 hours or until firm. Garnish with reserved pineapple. Store leftover gelatin in refrigerator.

Makes 12 servings

Prep Time: 10 minutes
Refrigerate Time: 4 hours 45 minutes

Tip

For a beautiful presentation at your next gathering, prepare as directed above and pour into your favorite individual dessert dishes. Each guest can then be served his or her own personal dessert.

Frozen Black-Bottom-Peanut Butter Pie

37 RITZ Crackers
6 tablespoons butter *or* margarine, melted
⅓ cup hot fudge dessert topping, heated slightly to soften
1 cup creamy peanut butter
1 cup cold milk
1 package (4-serving size) JELL-O Vanilla *or* Chocolate Flavor Instant Pudding & Pie Filling
1 tub (8 ounces) COOL WHIP Whipped Topping, thawed
Chopped peanuts (optional)

CRUSH crackers in zipper-style plastic bag with rolling pin or in food processor. Mix cracker crumbs and butter. Press onto bottom and up side of 9-inch pie plate; chill. Carefully spread fudge topping over crust.

BEAT peanut butter and milk in large bowl with wire whisk until blended. Add pudding mix. Beat with wire whisk 2 minutes or until well blended. Stir in ½ tub whipped topping. Spoon into crust. Spread remaining whipped topping over top.

FREEZE 4 hours. Sprinkle with chopped PLANTERS Peanuts.
Makes 8 servings

Great Substitute: *Try using chunky peanut butter instead of creamy for extra peanut flavor.*

Prep Time: 10 minutes plus freezing

Tip

To make an age old favorite combo, just substitute ⅓ cup strawberry preserves for the hot fudge and this luscious pie becomes a classic … Peanut Butter and Jelly Pie!

Special Occasions

Sparkling Fruit Tart

1 cup boiling water
1 package (4-serving size) JELL-O Brand Strawberry
 Flavor Gelatin
1 package (10 ounces) frozen strawberries in syrup
1 can (11 ounces) mandarin orange segments, drained
1 small banana, sliced
1 HONEY MAID Honey Graham Pie Crust (9 inch)

STIR boiling water into gelatin in large bowl at least
2 minutes until completely dissolved. Add frozen
strawberries. Stir until strawberries thaw and gelatin
becomes slightly thickened (consistency of unbeaten egg
whites).

ARRANGE orange and banana slices on bottom of crust.
Carefully spoon gelatin mixture over fruit.

REFRIGERATE 4 hours or until firm. Garnish with thawed
COOL WHIP Whipped Topping and fresh strawberry fans, if
desired.   *Makes 8 to 10 servings*

Prep Time: 15 minutes plus refrigerating

Sparkling Fruit Tart

Black & White Brownie Bottom Pudding Pie

>   4 squares BAKER'S Semi-Sweet Baking Chocolate
> ¼ cup (½ stick) butter *or* margarine
> ¾ cup sugar
> 2 eggs
> 1 teaspoon vanilla
> ½ cup flour
> 2½ cups cold milk
> 2 packages (4-serving size each) JELL-O White Chocolate *or* Vanilla Flavor Instant Pudding & Pie Filling

HEAT oven to 350°F (325°F for glass pie plate).

MICROWAVE chocolate and butter in small microwavable bowl on HIGH 2 minutes or until butter is melted. Stir until chocolate is completely melted.

STIR in sugar, eggs and vanilla. Blend in flour. Spread batter in greased 9-inch pie plate. Bake 25 minutes or until toothpick inserted in center comes out with fudgy crumbs. (DO NOT OVERBAKE.) Lightly press center with bottom of measuring cup or back of spoon to form slight depression. Cool on wire rack.

POUR milk into large bowl. Add pudding mixes. Beat with wire whisk 2 minutes or until well blended. Let stand 2 minutes. Spread over brownie pie. Top with thawed COOL WHIP Whipped Topping and grated chocolate, if desired. Refrigerate until ready to serve. *Makes 8 servings*

Great Substitute: *For an added crunch, stir in ½ cup chopped nuts after the flour and proceed as directed above.*

Prep Time: 15 minutes
Bake Time: 25 minutes

Black & White Brownie Bottom Pudding Pie

Tiramisu Toffee Trifle Pie

1½ tablespoons MAXWELL HOUSE Instant Coffee
¾ cup warm water
1 package (10.75 ounces) frozen pound cake, thawed, cut into 14 slices
1 package (8 ounces) PHILADELPHIA Cream Cheese, softened
½ cup powdered sugar
½ cup chocolate syrup
1 tub (12 ounces) COOL WHIP Whipped Topping, thawed
2 packages (1.4 ounces each) chocolate-covered English toffee bars, coarsely chopped (optional)

DISSOLVE instant coffee in water in small bowl; cool. Cut cake slices in half to form triangles. Arrange in 9-inch deep-dish pie plate. Drizzle coffee over cake.

BEAT cream cheese, sugar and chocolate syrup in large bowl with electric mixer on medium speed 2 minutes or until smooth. Gently stir in 2½ cups of the whipped topping. Spread over cake. Garnish with remaining whipped topping and chopped candy.

REFRIGERATE 4 hours or until firm.

Makes 8 to 10 servings

Helpful Hint: *Soften cream cheese in microwave on HIGH 15 to 20 seconds.*

Great Substitute: *Try this recipe with your favorite candy bar instead of the chocolate-covered English toffee bars.*

Prep Time: 30 minutes plus refrigerating

OREO *Black Forest Pie*

1 package (8 ounces) PHILADELPHIA Cream Cheese,
    softened
2½ cups cold milk
2 packages (4-serving size each) JELL-O Chocolate
    Flavor Instant Pudding & Pie Filling
1 OREO Pie Crust (9 inch)
1 cup cherry pie filling
1 cup thawed COOL WHIP Whipped Topping
    OREO Crunchies for garnish

BEAT cream cheese in large bowl with electric mixer on medium speed. Gradually beat in milk. Add pudding mixes. Beat on low speed 1 minute. Beat on medium speed 1 minute or until well blended. Spoon into crust.

REFRIGERATE 2 hours or until set. Just before serving, spoon pie filling over pudding. Garnish with whipped topping and crunchies. *Makes 8 servings*

Helpful Hint: *Soften cream cheese in microwave on HIGH 15 to 20 seconds.*

Prep Time: 20 minutes plus refrigerating

Tip

For a really decadent garnish, try dipping whole OREO Chocolate Sandwich Cookies into melted BAKER'S Semi-Sweet Chocolate, then refrigerate until set. Delicious!

Down Home Sour Cream Cheesecake

1 package (11.1 ounces) JELL-O No Bake Real Cheesecake
2 tablespoons sugar
6 tablespoons butter *or* margarine, melted
1 tablespoon water
1 cup cold milk
½ cup sour cream
2 teaspoons grated lemon peel
Lemon Sauce (optional)

STIR Crust Mix, sugar, butter and water thoroughly in 9-inch pie plate until crumbs are well moistened. First, firmly press crumbs against side of pie plate, using measuring cup or large spoon to shape edge. Next, firmly press remaining crumbs onto bottom.

POUR milk into large bowl. Add Filling Mix and sour cream. Beat with electric mixer on lowest speed until blended. Beat on medium speed 3 minutes. (Filling will be thick.) Gently stir in lemon peel and mix until completely blended. Spoon over crust.

REFRIGERATE at least 1 hour or until set. To serve, dip bottom of pan in hot water 30 seconds for easy cutting and serving. Serve with Lemon Sauce (recipe follows).

Makes 8 servings

Lemon Sauce: *Pour 1 cup cold milk into large bowl. Add 1 package (4-serving size) JELL-O Lemon Flavor Instant Pudding & Pie Filling. Beat with wire whisk 2 minutes or until well blended. Whisk in 3 tablespoons lemon juice.*

Special Extra: *Garnish with thawed COOL WHIP Whipped Topping and lemon slices.*

Prep Time: 15 minutes plus refrigerating

Down Home Sour Cream Cheesecake

Confetti Pie

1 cup boiling water
1 package (4-serving size) JELL-O Brand Lemon Flavor Gelatin
½ cup cold water
1 cup boiling water
1 package (4-serving size) JELL-O Brand Orange Flavor Gelatin
½ cup cold orange juice
2 cups thawed COOL WHIP Whipped Topping
⅓ cup multi-colored sprinkles
1 HONEY MAID Honey Graham Pie Crust (9 inch)

STIR 1 cup boiling water into lemon gelatin in medium bowl at least 2 minutes until completely dissolved. Stir in cold water. Pour into 8-inch square pan. Refrigerate 4 hours or until firm. Cut into ½-inch cubes.

STIR 1 cup boiling water into orange gelatin in large bowl at least 2 minutes until completely dissolved. Stir in orange juice. Refrigerate about 20 minutes or until slightly thickened (consistency of unbeaten egg whites). Gently stir in whipped topping. Gently stir in gelatin cubes and sprinkles. Refrigerate until mixture will mound. Pour into crust.

REFRIGERATE at least 4 hours or until firm. Garnish decoratively with additional whipped topping and sprinkles, if desired. *Makes 8 servings*

Great Substitutes: *Try Berry Blue or Lime Flavor Gelatin instead of Lemon Flavor when making the gelatin cubes.*

Prep Time: 15 minutes plus refrigerating

Spicey Apple Tart

4 cups thinly sliced peeled Granny Smith apples
²/₃ cup sugar
³/₄ cup apple juice *or* water
½ teaspoon ground cinnamon
2 tablespoons cornstarch
¼ cup cold water
1 package (4-serving size) JELL-O Brand Lemon Flavor Gelatin
1 HONEY MAID Honey Graham Pie Crust (9 inch)

MIX apples, sugar, apple juice and cinnamon in medium saucepan. Bring to boil over medium-high heat. Cook on medium heat about 5 minutes or until apples are tender. Mix cornstarch and water. Stir into apple mixture. Return to boil; boil 1 minute, stirring constantly. Remove from heat. Stir in gelatin until completely dissolved. Pour into crust.

REFRIGERATE 4 hours or until firm.   *Makes 8 servings*

Great Substitute: *Try NILLA Pie Crust (9 inch) instead of HONEY MAID Honey Graham Pie Crust.*

Special Extra: *Garnish with thawed COOL WHIP Whipped Topping.*

Prep Time: 15 minutes plus refrigerating

Tip

Rome apples may be substituted for the Granny Smith apples, if desired.

Ritzy Banana Cream Pie

37 RITZ Crackers
½ cup (1 stick) butter *or* margarine, divided
1 package (6 squares) BAKER'S Bittersweet Baking Chocolate, divided
2 large ripe bananas, sliced, divided
1½ cups cold milk
2 packages (4-serving size each) JELL-O Banana Cream Flavor Instant Pudding & Pie Filling
1 tub (8 ounces) COOL WHIP Whipped Topping, thawed
Chocolate-Dipped RITZ Crackers, for garnish

CRUSH crackers in zipper-style bag with rolling pin or in food processor. Melt 6 tablespoons butter. Mix cracker crumbs and butter. Press onto bottom and up side of 9-inch pie plate. Refrigerate until firm.

MICROWAVE 4 squares of the chocolate and remaining 2 tablespoons butter in small microwavable bowl on HIGH 2 minutes or until butter is melted. Stir until chocolate is completely melted. Carefully spread chocolate mixture over bottom and side of crust. Arrange ½ of banana slices on bottom and side of chocolate-coated crust.

POUR milk into medium bowl. Add pudding mixes. Beat with wire whisk 2 minutes or until well blended. (Mixture will be thick.) Gently fold in ½ tub whipped topping. Spoon into crust. Top with remaining banana slices. Spread remaining whipped topping on pie.

REFRIGERATE 4 hours or until set. Just before serving, garnish with Chocolate-Dipped RITZ Crackers.

Makes 8 servings

Chocolate-Dipped RITZ Crackers: *Microwave remaining 2 squares chocolate in small microwavable bowl on HIGH 1 to 2 minutes or until chocolate is almost melted. Stir until chocolate is completely melted. Dip each cracker halfway into melted chocolate; let excess chocolate drip off. Place on wax paper-lined cookie sheet. Refrigerate until chocolate is firm.*

Great Substitutes: *For variety try JELL-O Vanilla or Chocolate Flavor Instant Pudding & Pie Filling instead of Banana Cream Flavor.*

Prep Time: 15 minutes plus refrigerating

Decadent Chocolate Cream Pie

2 packages (4-serving size each) JELL-O Chocolate Flavor Cook & Serve Pudding & Pie Filling (not Instant)
3½ cups half-and-half
1 baked pastry shell (9 inch), cooled
1 tub (8 ounces) COOL WHIP Whipped Topping, thawed

STIR pudding mixes and half-and-half in medium saucepan with wire whisk until blended. Stirring constantly, cook over medium heat until mixture comes to full boil. Pour into pastry shell.

REFRIGERATE 3 hours or until set. Garnish pie with whipped topping.   *Makes 8 servings*

Great Substitute: *Use an OREO Pie Crust (9 inch) instead of a pastry shell. Garnish pie with chocolate shavings or chocolate sprinkles.*

Prep Time: 10 minutes plus refrigerating

Maple Praline Cheesecake

- 1 package (11.1 ounces) JELL-O Brand No Bake Real Cheesecake
- 2 tablespoons sugar
- 6 tablespoons butter *or* margarine, melted
- 1 tablespoon water
- 1⅓ cups cold milk
- ½ cup maple syrup
- ½ cup PLANTERS Pecan Halves *or* Pieces
- ½ cup firmly packed brown sugar
- 1 egg white

HEAT oven to 350°F.

STIR Crust Mix, sugar, butter and water thoroughly in 8- or 9-inch square baking pan until crumbs are well moistened. Firmly press crumbs onto bottom of pan, using small measuring cup.

POUR milk into large bowl. Add Filling Mix and syrup. Beat with electric mixer on lowest speed until blended. Beat on medium speed 3 minutes. (Filling will be thick.) Spoon over crust.

REFRIGERATE at least 1 hour or until set.

MIX pecans, brown sugar and egg white, stirring until well combined. Pour into greased 9-inch square baking pan. Bake 10 to 12 minutes or until browned and crunchy; cool. Using spatula, loosen nut mixture from pan and chop into small pieces. Just before serving, sprinkle over cheesecake. Cut cheesecake into squares.   *Makes 8 servings*

How To Serve: *To make cheesecake easier to serve, line 8- or 9-inch square pan with foil extending over edges to form handles. To serve, run knife around edges of pan to loosen cheesecake from sides. Lift cheesecake, using foil as handles, onto cutting board.*

Prep Time: 15 minutes plus refrigerating

Maple Praline Cheesecake

Sweet Indulgences

Strawberry Shortcakes

- ½ cup sugar
- 1 quart sliced strawberries (about 4 cups)
- 2⅓ cups BISQUICK Original Baking Mix
- ½ cup milk
- 3 tablespoons sugar
- 3 tablespoons butter *or* margarine, melted
- 1 tub (8 ounces) COOL WHIP Whipped Topping, thawed

HEAT oven to 425°F.

MIX ½ cup sugar into strawberries; set aside. Stir baking mix, milk, butter and 3 tablespoons sugar in bowl until soft dough forms. Drop by 6 spoonfuls onto ungreased cookie sheet.

BAKE 10 to 12 minutes or until golden brown. Split warm shortcakes; fill and top with strawberries and whipped topping.   *Makes 6 servings*

Prep Time: 6 minutes
Bake Time: 12 minutes

Strawberry Shortcake

Black & White Banana Pudding

1¾ **cups cold milk**
1 **package (4-serving size) JELL-O Chocolate Flavor Instant Pudding & Pie Filling**
24 **NILLA Chocolate Wafers** *or* **NILLA Wafers**
1 **large banana, sliced**
1 **tub (8 ounces) COOL WHIP Whipped Topping, thawed Finely chopped chocolate** *or* **sprinkles (optional)**

POUR milk into large bowl. Add pudding mix. Beat with wire whisk 2 minutes or until well blended. Let stand 5 minutes.

ARRANGE ½ of the cookies on bottom of 1 to 1½-quart serving bowl. Top with ½ of the pudding, ½ of the banana slices and ½ of the whipped topping. Repeat layers.

REFRIGERATE 3 hours or until ready to serve. Just before serving, garnish with chopped chocolate and additional banana slices dipped in lemon juice to prevent darkening, if desired. *Makes 4 to 6 servings*

Variation: *Substitute JELL-O Chocolate Flavor Sugar Free Instant Reduced Calorie Pudding & Pie Filling, COOL WHIP LITE Whipped Topping and fat free milk for regular JELL-O Instant Pudding & Pie Filling, COOL WHIP and milk.*

Prep Time: 20 minutes plus refrigerating

Tip

For a quick and easy seasonal look, just add a few drops of food coloring to the COOL WHIP *and voila! A festive look—orange for Halloween, red for Christmas, the sky's the limit.*

Raspberry-Topped White Chocolate Cheesecake

1 package (12 ounces) pound cake, cut into 12 slices
3 cups cold milk
1 package (4-serving size) JELL-O White Chocolate Flavor Instant Pudding & Pie Filling
1 package (4-serving size) JELL-O Cheesecake Flavor Instant Pudding & Pie Filling
2 cups fresh raspberries
⅔ cup boiling water
1 package (4-serving size) JELL-O Brand Raspberry Flavor Gelatin
COOL WHIP Whipped Topping, thawed (optional)

CUT pound cake slices in half to form triangles. Arrange cake triangles in bottom and up side of 9- or 10-inch springform pan.

POUR milk into large bowl. Add pudding mixes. Beat with wire whisk 2 minutes or until well blended. Spoon pudding mixture over cake in pan. Top with raspberries.

STIR boiling water into gelatin in medium bowl at least 2 minutes until completely dissolved. Refrigerate 30 minutes or until slightly thickened (consistency of unbeaten egg whites). Spoon evenly over raspberries.

REFRIGERATE 4 hours or until firm. Serve with whipped topping.   *Makes 12 servings*

Great Substitute: *Try JELL-O Brand Strawberry Flavor Gelatin and 2 cups sliced strawberries instead of Raspberry Flavor and raspberries.*

Prep Time: 20 minutes plus refrigerating

Layer After Layer Lemon Pie

⅓ cup strawberry jam
1 HONEY MAID Honey Graham Pie Crust (9 inch)
4 ounces PHILADELPHIA Cream Cheese, softened
1 tablespoon sugar
1 tub (8 ounces) COOL WHIP Whipped Topping, thawed, divided
1½ cups cold milk *or* half-and-half
2 packages (4-serving size each) JELL-O Lemon Flavor Instant Pudding & Pie Filling
2 teaspoons grated lemon peel

SPREAD jam gently onto bottom of pie crust. Mix cream cheese and sugar in large bowl with wire whisk until smooth. Gently stir in ½ of the whipped topping. Spread on top of jam.

POUR milk into large bowl. Add pudding mixes and lemon peel. Beat with wire whisk 1 minute. (Mixture will be thick.) Gently stir in remaining whipped topping. Spread over cream cheese layer.

REFRIGERATE 4 hours or until set. Garnish with additional whipped topping, if desired.   *Makes 8 servings*

Best of the Season: *For an extra-special fruity flavor, place 1 cup strawberries onto jam on bottom of crust; proceed as above.*

Helpful Hint: *Soften cream cheese in microwave on HIGH 15 to 20 seconds.*

Prep Time: 20 minutes plus refrigerating

Easy Cappuccino Cake

1 package (2-layer size) white cake mix
4 tablespoons MAXWELL HOUSE Instant Coffee,
    divided
¼ cup milk plus 1 tablespoon milk
4 squares BAKER'S Semi-Sweet Baking Chocolate,
    melted
2 tubs (8 ounces each) COOL WHIP Whipped Topping,
    thawed, divided

HEAT oven to 350°F.

PREPARE and bake cake mix as directed on package for 8- or 9-inch round pans, adding 2 tablespoons instant coffee to cake mix.

POUR ¼ cup milk and 1 tablespoon instant coffee into small bowl, stirring until coffee is dissolved. Slowly stir into melted chocolate until smooth. Cool completely. Gently stir in 1 tub whipped topping. Refrigerate 20 minutes, or until well chilled.

MEANWHILE, mix 1 tablespoon milk and remaining 1 tablespoon coffee until dissolved. Gently stir into remaining tub of whipped topping.

COVER one cake layer with chocolate mixture. Place second cake layer on top. Frost top and side of cake with coffee-flavored whipped topping. Refrigerate until ready to serve.   *Makes 12 servings*

Variation: *If desired, omit the coffee for a delicious plain chocolate filled layer cake.*

Prep Time: 25 minutes

Easy Cappuccino Cake

Triple Layer Pistachio Pie

2 squares BAKER'S Semi-Sweet Baking Chocolate, melted
¼ cup sweetened condensed milk
1 OREO Pie Crust (9 inch)
1¾ cups cold milk
2 packages (4-serving size each) JELL-O Pistachio Flavor Instant Pudding & Pie Filling
1 tub (8 ounces) COOL WHIP Whipped Topping, thawed

POUR chocolate and sweetened condensed milk into bowl; stir until smooth. Pour into crust. Refrigerate 10 minutes.

POUR milk into large bowl. Add pudding mixes. Beat with wire whisk 2 minutes or until well blended. (Mixture will be thick.) Spread 1½ cups of the pudding over chocolate in crust. Immediately stir ½ of the whipped topping into remaining pudding. Spread over pudding in crust. Top with remaining whipped topping.

REFRIGERATE 3 hours or until set. Garnish as desired.

Makes 8 servings

Great Substitute: *If you are a chocolate lover, simply substitute Chocolate Flavor Pudding for the Pistachio Flavor.*

Prep Time: 15 minutes plus refrigerating

Tip

To make this recipe have a real "WOW," simply drizzle with melted BAKER'S *chocolate.*

Super Luscious OREO *Cheesecake Pie*

4 ounces PHILADELPHIA Cream Cheese, softened
2 cups cold milk, divided
2 packages (4-serving size each) JELL-O Pistachio Flavor
    Instant Pudding & Pie Filling
1 tub (8 ounces) COOL WHIP Whipped Topping, thawed
1 package (8 ounces) Mini OREO Chocolate Sandwich
    Cookies, divided
1 OREO Pie Crust (9 inch)

BEAT cream cheese and ½ cup milk in large bowl with wire whisk until smooth. Add remaining 1½ cups milk and pudding mixes. Beat with wire whisk 2 minutes or until well blended. Stir in whipped topping until smooth and well blended. Reserving 20 cookies, gently stir remaining cookies into pudding mixture. Spoon into crust.

REFRIGERATE 4 hours or until set. Garnish by placing remaining cookies around edge of pie.   *Makes 8 servings*

Helpful Hint: *Soften cream cheese in microwave on HIGH 15 seconds.*

Great Substitute: *Prepare cheesecake as directed above, substituting 20 chopped or broken OREO Chocolate Sandwich Cookies for the Mini OREO Chocolate Sandwich Cookies, and stirring all cookies into the filling. Garnish as desired.*

CHIPS AHOY! Pistachio Cheesecake: *Prepare cheesecake as directed above, substituting NILLA Pie Crust for the OREO Pie Crust and 20 chopped or broken CHIPS AHOY! Chocolate Chip Cookies for the Mini OREO Chocolate Sandwich Cookies, and stirring all cookies into the filling. Garnish as desired.*

Prep Time: 10 minutes plus refrigerating

No Bake Frozen Chocolate Indulgence

1 package (11.4 ounces) JELL-O No Bake Chocolate Lover's Dessert
6 tablespoons butter *or* margarine, melted
1⅓ cups cold milk
¾ cup raspberry preserves
1 tub (8 ounces) EXTRA CREAMY COOL WHIP Whipped Topping *or* COOL WHIP Whipped Topping

STIR Crust Mix and butter thoroughly in 9-inch pie plate until crumbs are well moistened. First, firmly press crumbs against side of pie plate, using measuring cup or large spoon to shape edge. Next, firmly press remaining crumbs onto bottom.

POUR milk into large bowl. Add Filling Mix. Beat with electric mixer on lowest speed until blended. Beat on medium speed 3 minutes. (Filling will be thick.) Spoon into crust. Spread raspberry preserves evenly over filling. Top with whipped topping and drizzle with Topping.

FREEZE at least 4 hours or until firm. To serve, dip bottom of pan in hot water 30 seconds for easy cutting and serving.

Makes 8 servings

Great Substitute: *JELL-O No Bake Chocolate Silk Dessert can be substituted for the Chocolate Lover's Dessert by increasing cold milk to 1⅔ cups.*

Mini Chocolate Indulgence Treats: *Prepare as directed above, pressing prepared crumb mixture onto bottoms of 12 paper-lined muffin cups (about 1 heaping tablespoon per cup). Divide prepared filling among cups. Spread preserves and whipped topping over each dessert. Drizzle with Topping and freeze.*

Prep Time: 15 minutes plus freezing

Crème Caramel

**2 packages (4-serving size each) JELL-O Vanilla Flavor
Cook & Serve Pudding & Pie Filling (not Instant)**
1 quart milk *or* half-and-half
2 eggs, slightly beaten
1 teaspoon vanilla
¼ cup caramel dessert topping (optional)

STIR pudding mixes and milk with wire whisk in large saucepan until blended. Stirring constantly, cook over medium heat until mixture comes to full boil. Remove from heat.

STIR small amount of hot mixture into eggs in medium bowl until blended. Return mixture to saucepan and continue cooking over low heat 1 minute, stirring constantly. Stir in vanilla. Pour into bowl or 8 to 10 individual dessert dishes.

REFRIGERATE at least 3 hours. Drizzle with caramel topping.

Makes 8 to 10 servings

Note: *This recipe is best made with whole milk, but can be prepared with 2% reduced fat milk.*

Special Extra: *For an extra special twist, serve in goblets over fresh seasonal berries.*

Prep Time: 15 minutes plus refrigerating

Tip

This recipe goes to the next step when drizzled with both the caramel sauce and a rich chocolate sauce.

Holiday Poke Cake

2 baked 9-inch round white cake layers, cooled
2 cups boiling water, divided
1 package (4-serving size) JELL-O Brand Gelatin, any red flavor
1 package (4-serving size) JELL-O Brand Lime Flavor Gelatin
2 cups cold water
1 tub (8 ounces) COOL WHIP Whipped Topping, thawed

PLACE cake layers, top sides up, in 2 clean 9-inch round cake pans. Pierce cake with large fork at ½-inch intervals.

STIR 1 cup boiling water into both red and lime gelatin in separate bowls at least 2 minutes until completely dissolved. Carefully pour red gelatin over one cake layer and lime gelatin over second cake layer. Refrigerate 3 hours.

DIP 1 cake pan in warm water 10 seconds; unmold onto serving plate. Spread about 1 cup whipped topping on cake layer. Unmold second cake layer; carefully place on first cake layer. Frost top and side of cake with remaining whipped topping.

REFRIGERATE 1 hour or until ready to serve. Garnish with fresh fruit, if desired. *Makes 12 servings*

Variation: *To make this recipe for any holiday, just substitute the appropriate flavor JELL-O Brand Gelatin.*

Prep Time: 30 minutes plus refrigerating

Layered Mint-Chocolate Loaf

2 cups boiling water
1 package (8-serving size) *or* 2 packages (4-serving size each) JELL-O Brand Lime Flavor Gelatin
1¼ cups cold water
¼ teaspoon peppermint extract
2 cups thawed COOL WHIP Whipped Topping
8 OREO Chocolate Sandwich Cookies, chopped

STIR boiling water into gelatin in large bowl at least 2 minutes until completely dissolved. Stir in cold water and peppermint extract. Refrigerate about 1½ hours or until slightly thickened (consistency of unbeaten egg whites). Gently stir in whipped topping. Carefully spoon ½ of the gelatin mixture into 9×5-inch loaf pan which has been sprayed with no stick cooking spray. Sprinkle with ½ of the cookies. Repeat layers, ending with gelatin mixture.

REFRIGERATE about 4 hours or until firm. Unmold. Garnish with additional whipped topping and cookies, if desired.

Great Substitute: *Omit peppermint extract. Substitute 8 MYSTIC MINT Chocolate Sandwich Cookies.*

Prep Time: 15 minutes plus refrigerating

Tip

This recipe easily takes on a holiday look by simply sprinkling the COOL WHIP *garnish with red sprinkles.*

Simple Pleasures

Chocolaty-Rich Hot Cocoa

   **1 package (4-serving size) JELL-O Chocolate Flavor
       Cook & Serve Pudding & Pie Filling (not Instant)**
1 ½ **quarts milk**
   ½ **cup BAKER'S Semi-Sweet Chocolate Chunks**
   ½ **teaspoon vanilla
       Thawed COOL WHIP Whipped Topping *or*
       JET-PUFFED Miniature Marshmallows (optional)**

STIR pudding mix and milk in medium saucepan with wire whisk until blended. Stirring constantly, cook over medium heat until mixture comes to full boil. Remove from heat. Add chocolate chunks and vanilla. Stir with wire whisk until well blended.

POUR into mugs and garnish with a dollop of whipped topping or several marshmallows. Serve immediately.

Makes 6 servings

Helpful Hint: *Mixture will thicken as it stands. To thin, just add more milk and reheat.*

Prep Time: 10 minutes

*Chocolaty-Rich Hot Cocoa and
Glazed Lemon Cake (page 60)*

Glazed Lemon Cake

> **1 package (2-layer size) yellow cake mix**
> **1 package (4-serving size) JELL-O Brand Lemon Flavor Gelatin**
> **4 eggs**
> **⅔ cup hot water**
> **⅔ cup oil**
> **¼ cup COUNTRY TIME Lemonade Flavor Drink Mix**
> **¼ cup water**
> **1 cup powdered sugar**

HEAT oven to 350°F.

STIR cake mix, gelatin, eggs, water and oil in large bowl. Beat with electric mixer on low speed 1 minute. Beat on medium speed 4 minutes. Pour into greased and floured 12-cup fluted tube pan.

BAKE 35 to 40 minutes or until toothpick inserted in center comes out clean. Cool in pan 5 minutes. Invert onto wire rack. Cool 5 minutes.

STIR lemonade mix and water in medium bowl. Stir in powdered sugar with wire whisk until well blended to make glaze.

PIERCE warm cake with large fork or skewer at ½-inch intervals. Gradually spoon glaze over cake.

Makes 16 servings

Great Substitute: *Use lemon flavor cake mix instead of yellow cake mix.*

Prep Time: 30 minutes
Bake Time: 40 minutes

Chocolate Mallow Cookie Pie

    2 cups JET-PUFFED Miniature Marshmallows
    2 tablespoons milk
 2½ cups thawed COOL WHIP Whipped Topping, divided
    2 cups cold milk
    2 packages (4-serving size) JELL-O Chocolate Flavor
        Instant Pudding & Pie Filling
    1 OREO Pie Crust (9 inch)
   14 NILLA wafers, chopped
      Chocolate Topping (optional)

MICROWAVE marshmallows and 2 tablespoons milk in medium microwavable bowl on HIGH 1 minute, stirring after 30 seconds. Stir until marshmallows are melted. Refrigerate 15 minutes to cool. Gently stir in 1 cup whipped topping.

POUR 2 cups milk into large bowl. Add pudding mixes. Beat with wire whisk 2 minutes or until well blended. Gently stir in remaining whipped topping. Spoon into crust. Arrange cookies over top. Spread marshmallow mixture over cookies. Drizzle with Chocolate Topping.

REFRIGERATE 4 hours or until set. *Makes 8 servings*

Chocolate Topping: *Microwave 2 squares BAKER'S Semi-Sweet Baking Chocolate in heavy zipper-style plastic sandwich bag on HIGH 1 to 2 minutes or until chocolate is almost melted. Add 2 teaspoons softened butter; gently squeeze bag until chocolate and butter are completely melted. Fold down top of bag; snip tiny piece off 1 corner from bottom. Drizzle chocolate mixture over top of pie. Refrigerate as directed above.*

Prep Time: 30 minutes plus refrigerating

Easy 5-Minute Desserts

Warm Cinnamon Bun Pudding: *Prepare 1 package (4-serving size) Vanilla Flavor JELL-O Instant Pudding & Pie filling as directed on package. Stir in ¹/₂ teaspoon ground cinnamon. Spoon into microwavable dessert dishes. Swirl 1 tablespoon caramel dessert topping into each serving. Microwave each serving (¹/₂ cup) on HIGH 35 seconds or until pudding is heated through. Top each with a dollop of thawed COOL WHIP Whipped Topping and sprinkle with chopped toasted PLANTERS Pecan Pieces. Stir and serve immediately. Makes 4 servings*

Eggnog Custard Cups: *Prepare 1 package (4-serving size) Vanilla Flavor JELL-O Instant Pudding & Pie Filling as directed on package substituting half-and-half for milk. Stir in ¹/₄ teaspoon ground nutmeg and ¹/₂ teaspoon rum extract. Spoon into individual dessert dishes. Top each with a dollop of thawed COOL WHIP Whipped Topping and sprinkle with additional nutmeg, if desired. Makes 4 servings*

Mocha Cups: *Prepare 1 package (4-serving size) Chocolate Flavor JELL-O Instant Pudding & Pie Filling as directed on package. Stir in 2 teaspoons instant espresso powder. Gently stir in 1 cup thawed COOL WHIP Whipped Topping. Spoon into individual dessert dishes. Top each with a dollop of thawed COOL WHIP Whipped Topping and sprinkle with ground cinnamon, if desired. Makes 4 servings*

"No Pumpkin" Pie Cups: *Prepare 1 package (4-serving size) Vanilla Flavor JELL-O Instant Pudding & Pie Filling as directed on package. Stir in 1 teaspoon pumpkin pie spice and 1 cup chopped NABISCO Old Fashioned Ginger Snaps. Spoon into individual dessert dishes. Top each with a dollop of thawed COOL WHIP Whipped Topping, if desired. Makes 4 servings*

Citrus Coconut Squares

2 cups LORNA DOONE Shortbread crumbs
¼ cup sugar
⅓ cup butter *or* margarine, melted
⅔ cup boiling orange juice
**1 package (4-serving size) Orange *or* Lemon Flavor
JELL-O Brand Gelatin**
**½ cup cold orange juice
Ice cubes**
**1 tub (12 ounces) COOL WHIP Whipped Topping,
thawed, divided**
½ cup BAKER'S ANGEL FLAKE Coconut, toasted

MIX crumbs, sugar and butter with fork in 13×9-inch baking pan until crumbs are well moistened. Press firmly onto bottom of pan. Refrigerate until ready to fill.

STIR boiling juice into gelatin in large bowl at least 2 minutes until completely dissolved. Mix cold juice and ice cubes to make 1¼ cups. Add to gelatin, stirring until slightly thickened (consistency of unbeaten egg whites). Remove any remaining ice. Stir in 3½ cups of the whipped topping with wire whisk until smooth. Pour over crust.

REFRIGERATE 3 hours or until firm. Just before serving, spread remaining whipped topping over gelatin mixture. Sprinkle coconut on top. Cut into squares.

Makes 15 to 18 servings

Best of Season: *For a great twist, add 1 cup of seasonal berries to the thickened gelatin and proceed as directed.*

Prep Time: 15 minutes
Refrigerate Time: 3 hours

Creamy Tropical Island Squares

2 cups NABISCO Old Fashioned Ginger Snaps, finely crushed
¼ cup sugar
⅓ cup butter *or* margarine, melted
1½ cups boiling water
1 package (8-serving size) *or* 2 packages (4-serving size each) JELL-O Brand Lemon Flavor Gelatin
1 can (20 ounces) crushed pineapple in juice
Cold water
1 package (8 ounces) PHILADELPHIA Cream Cheese, softened
1 tub (8 ounces) COOL WHIP Whipped Topping, thawed
1 cup chopped strawberries
1 cup toasted BAKER'S ANGEL FLAKE Coconut (optional)

MIX ginger snap crumbs, sugar and butter in 13×9-inch baking pan until crumbs are well moistened. Press firmly onto bottom of pan. Refrigerate until ready to fill.

STIR boiling water into gelatin in large bowl at least 2 minutes until completely dissolved. Drain pineapple, reserving juice. Set aside pineapple. Mix juice and water to make 2 cups. Stir into gelatin. Whisk in cream cheese until well blended. Refrigerate about 1½ hours or until thickened (spoon drawn through leaves definite impression).

STIR whipped topping into gelatin mixture with wire whisk until smooth. Pour mixture over crust.

REFRIGERATE 3 hours or until firm. Top with pineapple and strawberries. Sprinkle with coconut.   *Makes 15 servings*

Helpful Hint: *Soften cream cheese in microwave on HIGH 15 to 20 seconds.*

Great Substitute: *Try JELL-O Brand Orange Flavor Gelatin instead of Lemon Flavor.*

Prep Time: 15 minutes plus refrigerating

Yummy JELL-O *Peanut Butter Pudding Treats*

Peanut Butter Dream Cups: *Prepare 1 package (4-serving size) JELL-O Chocolate or Vanilla Flavor Instant Pudding as directed on package. Mix in $\frac{1}{2}$ cup peanut butter; beat until well combined. Spoon mixture into individual serving cups. Top with thawed COOL WHIP Whipped Topping. Makes 4 to 6 servings*

Peanut Butter Cloud Cups: *Prepare 1 package (4-serving size) JELL-O Chocolate or Vanilla Flavor Instant Pudding as directed on package. Mix in $\frac{1}{2}$ cup peanut butter; beat until well combined. Fold in $\frac{1}{2}$ tub of thawed COOL WHIP Whipped Topping, stirring gently. Spoon mixture into individual serving cups. Top with remaing COOL WHIP. Makes 4 to 6 servings*

Fluffy Monkey Dream Cups: *Prepare 1 package (4-serving size) JELL-O Chocolate or Vanilla Flavor Instant Pudding as directed on package. Mix in $\frac{1}{2}$ cup peanut butter; beat until well combined. Fold in $\frac{1}{2}$ tub of thawed COOL WHIP Whipped Topping, stirring gently. Spoon mixture into individual serving cups, layering with chopped bananas and peanuts. Top with COOL WHIP. Makes 4 to 6 servings*

Peanut Butter and Jelly Parfaits: *Prepare 1 package (4-serving size) JELL-O Vanilla Flavor Instant Pudding as directed on package. Mix in $\frac{1}{2}$ cup peanut butter; beat until well combined. Layer mixture in individual serving cups or parfait glasses with spoonfuls of your favorite jelly and thawed COOL WHIP Whipped Topping, alternating layers. Top with final layer of COOL WHIP. Makes 4 to 6 servings*

Peanut Butter and Jelly-Filled Cups: *Prepare 1 package (4-serving size) JELL-O Chocolate or Vanilla Flavor Instant Pudding as directed on package. Add $\frac{1}{2}$ cup peanut butter; beat until well combined. Spoon mixture into individual serving cups. Place spoonful of your favorite jelly in center of cup, and cover with another spoonful of pudding mixture. Makes 4 to 6 servings*

Orange Mousse with Strawberry Sauce

1½ cups boiling water
1 package (8-serving size) *or* 2 packages (4-serving size each) JELL-O Brand Orange Flavor Gelatin
2 teaspoons grated orange peel (optional)
1 cup cold water
¾ cup cold orange juice
1 tub (8 ounces) COOL WHIP Whipped Topping, thawed
1 package (10 ounces) frozen strawberries *or* raspberries in syrup, thawed, puréed in blender

STIR boiling water into gelatin and orange peel in large bowl at least 2 minutes until gelatin is completely dissolved. Stir in cold water and orange juice. Refrigerate about 1¼ hours or until slightly thickened (consistency of unbeaten egg whites).

STIR in whipped topping with wire whisk until smooth. Pour into 6-cup mold which has been sprayed with no stick cooking spray.

REFRIGERATE 3 hours or until firm. Unmold. Serve with puréed strawberries.   *Makes 12 servings*

How To Unmold: *Dip mold in warm water for about 15 seconds. Gently pull gelatin from around edges with moist fingers. Place moistened serving plate on top of mold. Invert mold and plate; holding mold and plate together, shake slightly to loosen. Gently remove mold and center gelatin on plate.*

For individual servings: *Pour mousse mixture into 12 (6-ounce) custard cups, filling each about ¾ full.*

Lemon Mousse: *Substitute JELL-O Brand Lemon Flavor Gelatin and lemon peel for the Orange Flavor Gelatin and orange peel.*

Prep Time: 15 minutes plus refrigerating

Orange Mousse with Strawberry Sauce

Easy Rocky Road Fudge

1 package (6-serving size) JELL-O Chocolate Flavor Cook & Serve Pudding & Pie Filling (not Instant)
¼ cup milk
3 tablespoons butter *or* margarine
2¼ cups powdered sugar
½ cup chopped PLANTERS Walnuts
½ cup JET-PUFFED Miniature Marshmallows

STIR pudding mix and milk in medium microwavable bowl with wire whisk 2 minutes or until well blended. Add butter. Microwave on HIGH 1 minute; stir. Microwave 45 seconds longer or until mixture just starts to boil around edge. Beat in sugar with electric mixer. Stir in walnuts and marshmallows. Spread evenly into 8×4-inch foil-lined loaf pan.

REFRIGERATE about 1 hour.

Storage Know-How: *Store in tightly covered container in the refrigerator.*

Great Substitutes: *Use JELL-O Vanilla Flavor Cook & Serve Pudding instead of Chocolate Flavor. Replace walnuts and marshmallows with ½ cup chopped toasted almonds and ½ cup chopped dried mixed fruit bits.*

Prep Time: 15 minutes plus refrigerating

Tip

This recipe is great for gift giving around the holidays. Place in a decorative seasonal tin, or line a box with waxed paper—sure to please anyone on your list!

Easy Rocky Road Fudge

Creamy Peach-Raspberry Melba

¾ cup boiling water
1 package (4-serving size) JELL-O Brand Raspberry
   Flavor Gelatin
½ cup cold water
   Ice cubes
¼ teaspoon almond extract
1 tub (8 ounces) COOL WHIP Whipped Topping, thawed
1 medium peach, peeled and diced

STIR boiling water into gelatin in medium bowl at least
2 minutes until completely dissolved. Mix cold water and
ice to make 1 cup. Add to gelatin, stirring until ice is melted.
Stir in almond extract. Refrigerate 20 minutes or until
slightly thickened (consistency of unbeaten egg whites).
Gently stir in whipped topping. Gently stir in peach. Spoon
into dessert dishes.

REFRIGERATE at least 30 minutes or until set. Garnish with
additional whipped topping, if desired.

Makes 8 servings

Special Extra: *Garnish with fresh raspberries.*

Prep Time: 15 minutes plus refrigerating

Easy Mallow Brulée

2 cups cold half-and-half
1 package (4-serving size) JELL-O Vanilla Flavor Instant
   Pudding & Pie Filling
1 cup JET-PUFFED Miniature Marshmallows

POUR half-and-half into large bowl. Add pudding mix. Beat
with wire whisk 2 minutes or until well blended. Pour into
4 (6-ounce) custard cups.

HEAT broiler. Top each cup with marshmallows. Broil about 6 to 8 inches from broiler, about 1 to 2 minutes or until marshmallows are golden brown, watching carefully.

Makes 4 servings

Great Substitute: *Try using JELL-O Lemon or Banana Flavor Instant Pudding instead of Vanilla Flavor.*

Prep Time: 10 minutes

Cherry Pie Squares

> 1 package (12 ounces) pound cake, cut into 10 slices
> 1 can (21 ounces) cherry pie filling
> 2¼ cups cold milk
> 2 packages (4-serving size each) JELL-O Vanilla *or* Lemon Flavor Instant Pudding & Pie Filling
> 1 tub (8 ounces) COOL WHIP Whipped Topping, thawed

ARRANGE cake slices in bottom of 13×9-inch baking pan. Top with pie filling.

POUR milk into large bowl. Add pudding mixes. Beat with wire whisk 2 minutes or until well blended. Gently stir in 1 cup of the whipped topping. Spoon mixture over pie filling in pan. Top with remaining whipped topping.

REFRIGERATE until ready to serve or overnight. Garnish as desired.

Makes 15 servings

Make-Ahead: *This recipe is great for a crowd and is even better when prepared the night before!*

Prep Time: 10 minutes

Fun Family Treats

Creamy Orange Cookie Cups

  1¼ cups boiling water
    1 package (4-serving size) JELL-O Brand Orange Flavor
      Gelatin
    1 pint vanilla ice cream (2 cups)
  16 NILLA Wafers, divided

STIR boiling water into gelatin in medium bowl at least
2 minutes until completely dissolved. Stir in ice cream until
melted. Place 1 cookie into each of 8 small cups. Pour
gelatin into cups.

REFRIGERATE 2 hours or until firm. Garnish with remaining
cookies and thawed COOL WHIP Whipped Topping, if
desired.   *Makes 8 servings*

Great Substitute: *Try NILLA Chocolate Wafers instead of the
NILLA Wafers.*

Prep Time: 5 minutes plus refrigerating

Creamy Orange Cookie Cups

Magical Marshmallow Carpets

1 package (8-serving size) *or* 2 packages (4-serving size each) JELL-O Brand Gelatin, any flavor
1 cup warm water
3 cups JET-PUFFED Miniature Marshmallows *or* 12 JET-PUFFED Marshmallows

LIGHTLY GREASE 13×9-inch baking pan with no stick cooking spray.

STIR gelatin and water in medium microwavable bowl. Microwave on HIGH 2½ minutes; stir until dissolved.

STIR in marshmallows. Microwave on HIGH 2 minutes or until marshmallows are partially melted. Stir mixture slowly until marshmallows are completely melted. Pour mixture into pan.

REFRIGERATE 1 hour or until set. Cut gelatin into 2¼×4¼-inch rectangles. With marshmallow layer on top, cut small slits on each side of the rectangles to form "carpet fringes." Garnish each "carpet" with multicolored sprinkles, if desired.   *Makes 16 pieces*

Prep Time: 10 minutes plus refrigerating

Tip

For different shapes, use cookie cutters to make a desired look.

Applesauce Yogurt Delight

1 cup boiling water
1 package (4-serving size) JELL-O Brand Gelatin, any red flavor
¾ cup cold applesauce
¼ teaspoon ground cinnamon
½ cup BREYERS Vanilla Lowfat Yogurt

STIR boiling water into gelatin in medium bowl at least 2 minutes until completely dissolved. Measure ¾ cup; stir in applesauce and cinnamon. Pour into bowl or 4 dessert dishes. Refrigerate about 15 minutes or until set but not firm.

REFRIGERATE remaining gelatin until slightly thickened (consistency of unbeaten egg whites). Mix in yogurt; spoon over gelatin in bowl.

REFRIGERATE 2 hours or until set.   *Makes 4 servings*

Variation: *This recipe can be made with JELL-O Brand Sugar Free Low Calorie Gelatin with superb results!*

Prep Time: 15 minutes plus refrigerating

Tip

Make this recipe in paper cups … great for a school or office "on-the-go" snack.

Frozen NUTTER BUTTER *Peanut Butter Dessert*

1 package (16.1 ounces) JELL-O No Bake Peanut Butter Cup Dessert
6 tablespoons butter *or* margarine, melted
1 package (16 ounces) NUTTER BUTTER Peanut Butter Sandwich Cookies, divided
1⅓ cups cold milk
1 tub (8 ounces) COOL WHIP Whipped Topping, thawed

PLACE Topping Pouch in large bowl of boiling water; set aside.

LINE 8-inch square baking pan with foil extending over edges to form handles.

STIR Crust Mix and butter thoroughly in medium bowl until crumbs are well moistened. Firmly press crumbs onto bottom of pan, using small measuring cup. Using approximately 20 sandwich cookies, line sides of pan with cookies in upright position. Chop or crush remaining cookies into small bite-size pieces. Set aside.

POUR milk into medium bowl. Add Filling Mix and Peanut Butter. Beat with electric mixer on lowest speed 30 seconds. Beat on highest speed 3 minutes. DO NOT UNDERBEAT. (Filling will be thick.) Gently stir whipped topping into peanut butter mixture until completely mixed. Gently stir in reserved cookie pieces. Carefully spoon mixture into pan. Smooth top with spatula.

REMOVE pouch from water. Knead pouch 60 seconds until fluid and no longer lumpy. Pour topping over filling. Tilt pan to evenly cover filling. (Topping will harden during freezing.)

FREEZE 2 hours or until firm. To serve, lift from pan, using foil as handles, onto cutting board. Remove foil. Cut into squares.   *Makes 8 servings*

Frozen NUTTER BUTTER Peanut Butter Pops: *Prepare crust as directed above, pressing crumbs onto bottoms of 12 paper-lined muffin cups. Prepare filling as directed above omitting whipped topping and chopped cookies. Divide mixture among cups. Prepare topping as directed above and drizzle over each cup. Press 1 NUTTER BUTTER Peanut Butter Sandwich Cookie halfway into each cup to serve as handle. Freeze 2 hours or until firm.*

Prep Time: 15 minutes plus freezing

Fun Party Waffles

12 frozen Belgian waffles
1 tub (8 ounces) COOL WHIP Whipped Topping *or*
1 package (6 ounces) COOL WHIP Squeeze
Whipped Topping, thawed
Multi-colored sprinkles

HEAT waffles as directed on package.

GARNISH waffles with whipped topping. Top with sprinkles.
Makes 12 servings

Great Substitutes: *Instead of sprinkles, top each waffle with assorted fresh fruit (such as blueberries, sliced strawberries and kiwi), chopped toasted nuts, chopped candy pieces (such as chocolate-covered English toffee bars) or chocolate syrup.*

Prep Time: 10 minutes

Super Cherry Cola Floats

1 cup boiling water
1 package (4-serving size) JELL-O Brand Cherry Flavor
Gelatin
1¼ cups cold cola
1 pint vanilla ice cream (2 cups)

STIR boiling water into gelatin in medium bowl 2 minutes until completely dissolved. Stir in cola. Refrigerate 20 to 30 minutes or until slightly thickened (consistency of unbeaten egg whites). Reserve ½ cup gelatin.

PLACE ½ cup ice cream into each of 4 tall ice cream soda glasses. Top with thickened gelatin mixture.

BEAT reserved ½ cup gelatin mixture with electric mixer on medium speed until light and fluffy. Spoon into each glass.

REFRIGERATE 2 hours or until firm.   *Makes 4 servings*

Special Extra: *Garnish each float with a maraschino cherry and sprinkles.*

Prep Time: 15 minutes plus refrigerating

Tip

This recipe tastes great with root beer too!

Super Cherry Cola Float

Chewy Fruit & Nut Bars

2 cups LORNA DOONE Shortbread crumbs
5 tablespoons butter *or* margarine, melted
1 cup boiling water
**2 packages (4-serving size each) JELL-O Brand Apricot
    or Peach Flavor Gelatin**
½ cup light corn syrup
1 cup chopped toasted PLANTERS Slivered Almonds

STIR crumbs and butter in 9-inch square baking pan until crumbs are well moistened, reserving ½ cup crumb mixture. Firmly press remaining crumbs onto bottom of pan. Refrigerate until ready to fill.

STIR boiling water into gelatin in large bowl at least 2 minutes until completely dissolved. Stir in corn syrup. Refrigerate 15 minutes or until slightly thickened (consistency of unbeaten egg whites). Stir in almonds. Pour into pan over crust. Sprinkle with remaining crumbs.

REFRIGERATE 3 hours or until firm. Cut into bars.

Makes 20 bars

Great Substitute: *Use JELL-O Brand Orange Flavor Gelatin instead of Apricot Flavor. Reduce almonds to ½ cup and add ½ cup chopped dried apricots.*

Prep Time: 15 minutes plus refrigerating

Tip

Two cups of HONEY MAID *Graham Cracker Crumbs may be substituted for the* LORNA DOONE *Shortbread Crumbs.*

Chewy Fruit & Nut Bars

Easy Lemon Pudding Cookies

1 cup BISQUICK Original Baking Mix
1 package (4-serving size) JELL-O Lemon Flavor Instant Pudding & Pie Filling
½ teaspoon ground ginger (optional)
1 egg, lightly beaten
¼ cup vegetable oil
Sugar
3 squares BAKER'S Premium White Baking Chocolate, melted

HEAT oven to 350°F.

STIR baking mix, pudding mix and ginger in medium bowl. Mix in egg and oil until well blended. (Mixture will be stiff.) With hands, roll cookie dough into 1-inch diameter balls. Place balls 2 inches apart on lightly greased cookie sheets. Dip flat-bottom glass into sugar. Press glass onto each dough ball and flatten into ¼-inch-thick cookie.

BAKE 10 minutes or until edges are golden brown. Immediately remove from cookie sheets. Cool on wire racks. Drizzle cookies with melted white chocolate.

Makes about 20 cookies

How To Melt Chocolate: *Microwave 3 squares BAKER'S Premium White Baking Chocolate in heavy zipper-style plastic sandwich bag on HIGH 1 to 1½ minutes or until chocolate is almost melted. Gently knead bag until chocolate is completely melted. Fold down top of bag; snip tiny piece off 1 corner from bottom. Holding top of bag tightly, drizzle chocolate through opening across tops of cookies.*

Prep Time: 10 minutes
Bake Time: 10 minutes

JELL-O *Yogurt Parfaits*

2 cups boiling water, divided
1 package (4-serving size) JELL-O Brand Gelatin, any red flavor
1 container (8 ounces) BREYERS Vanilla Lowfat Yogurt, divided
1 cup cold water, divided
1 package (4-serving size) JELL-O Brand Orange Flavor Gelatin

STIR 1 cup boiling water into red gelatin in medium bowl at least 2 minutes or until completely dissolved. Remove ½ cup gelatin to small bowl. Stir in ½ of the yogurt. Stir ½ cup cold water into other bowl. Refrigerate both bowls 15 to 20 minutes or until slightly thickened (consistency of unbeaten egg whites).

SPOON creamy red gelatin mixture evenly into 4 dessert glasses. Refrigerate 10 minutes or until thickened (spoon drawn through leaves a definite impression). Top each with clear red gelatin. Refrigerate until thickened.

MEANWHILE, repeat procedure with orange gelatin and remaining ingredients.

REFRIGERATE 3 hours or until firm.   *Makes 4 servings*

Great Substitute: *For a fun holiday treat, substitute Lime Flavor Gelatin for the Orange Flavor Gelatin. Garnish each serving with a dollop of thawed COOL WHIP Whipped Topping.*

Prep Time: 10 minutes plus refrigerating

Rocky Road Icebox Cake

3½ cups JET-PUFFED Miniature Marshmallows, divided
2 tablespoons milk
3 cups half-and-half *or* milk
2 packages (4-serving size each) JELL-O Chocolate Flavor Instant Pudding & Pie Filling
1 tub (8 ounces) COOL WHIP Whipped Topping, thawed, divided
5 or more whole HONEY MAID Honey Grahams, broken into pieces
1 jar (11.75 ounces) hot fudge topping
1 cup PLANTERS COCKTAIL Peanuts

LINE 9×5-inch loaf pan with foil extending over edges to form handles. Spray foil with no stick cooking spray.

MICROWAVE 3 cups marshmallows and 2 tablespoons milk in medium microwavable bowl 1 to 2 minutes or until almost melted. Stir until completely melted; cool.

POUR half-and-half into large bowl. Add pudding mixes. Beat with wire whisk 2 minutes or until well blended. (Mixture will be thick.) Gently stir in 1 cup whipped topping. Stir remaining whipped topping into cooled marshmallows.

LINE bottom of prepared pan with ⅓ of the honey graham crackers to form crust. Spread with ⅓ jar of hot fudge topping. Sprinkle with ⅓ cup peanuts. Spoon ½ of the pudding mixture over peanuts. Spoon ½ of the marshmallow mixture over pudding. Smooth with spatula. Repeat layers. Freeze at least 4 hours or until firm.

Makes 8 to 10 servings

How To Serve: *Lift dessert from pan, using foil as handles, onto cutting board. Remove foil. Let stand at room temperature 10 minutes before slicing. Top dessert with remaining peanuts, marshmallows and honey graham crackers. Drizzle remaining hot fudge sauce on top. Run knife under hot water and dry with towel for easier cutting.*

Prep Time: 15 minutes plus freezing

Rocky Road Icebox Cake

Monkey Shake

2 cups cold milk
1 ripe banana
1 package (4-serving size) JELL-O Chocolate Flavor
    Instant Pudding & Pie Filling
2 cups crushed ice

POUR milk into blender container. Add banana, pudding mix and ice; cover. Blend on high speed 15 seconds or until smooth. Serve at once.   *Makes 4 servings*

How To: *Mixture will thicken as it stands. To thin just add more milk, $\frac{1}{4}$ cup at a time for desired thickness.*

Prep Time: 10 minutes

Key Lime Smoothie

$\frac{1}{2}$ cup boiling water
1 package (4-serving size) JELL-O Brand Lime Flavor
    Gelatin
1 cup ice cubes
    Cold water
$1\frac{1}{2}$ cups thawed COOL WHIP Whipped Topping

STIR boiling water into gelatin in medium bowl at least 2 minutes until completely dissolved. Mix ice and enough cold water to make $1\frac{1}{2}$ cups.

POUR gelatin, ice water and whipped topping into blender container; cover. Blend on medium speed until smooth. Serve immediately.   *Makes 4 servings*

Great Substitute: *Try any flavor JELL-O Brand Gelatin for a delicious treat!*

Prep Time: 10 minutes

Left to right: Key Lime Smoothie and Monkey Shake

Easy JELL-O *Popcorn Balls*

¼ **cup (½ stick) butter *or* margarine**
**1 bag (10½ ounces) JET-PUFFED Miniature
    Marshmallows**
**1 package (4-serving size) JELL-O Brand Gelatin, any
    flavor**
3 quarts (12 cups) popped popcorn
1 cup PLANTERS COCKTAIL Peanuts (optional)

MICROWAVE butter and marshmallows in large
microwavable bowl on HIGH 1½ to 2 minutes or until
marshmallows are puffed. Stir in gelatin until well mixed.

POUR marshmallow mixture over popcorn and peanuts in
large bowl. Mix lightly until well coated. Shape into 15 balls
or other shapes with greased or wet hands.

Makes about 15 servings

Candy Corn Popcorn Balls: *Prepare Popcorn Balls as
directed above using JELL-O Orange Flavor Gelatin and
substituting 1 cup candy corn for the peanuts.*

Prep Time: 20 minutes

Tip

*Wrap popcorn balls in plastic wrap for great
take-along snacks.*

Index